Well D...

Guide &

Roly Smith

A
E

1910 2010

GUIDING - A CHALLENGE

HIGH PEAK
100

Buxton

IN LOVING
MEMORY

What are well dressings?

The well dressings of the Peak District attract thousands of visitors to local villages and towns throughout the summer. Visitors come to marvel at their intricate and colourful designs, each one different from the other and all done by local people usually using purely natural, locally-sourced materials.

Originally found only in the villages of the White Peak, they now take place in over 80 towns and villages in and around the Peak District (check with the local Tourist Information Centre for dates).

Throughout the summer, each village takes it in turn to decorate their wells or springs with these intricate floral icons, which often coincide with the village Wakes, or Patron Saint's, week.

It is thought that the custom originated in Pagan times as a thanksgiving for the gift of water, but the custom was later adopted by Christianity, and the first recorded historical examples took place at Tissington in 1758.

Most modern well dressings have a Christian or biblical message, but others use more modern topics or anniversaries. Occasionally the dressings appear at the village taps (pumps or fountains) to celebrate the arrival of piped water, and in this case they are known as tap dressings. Youlgrave and Wirksworth are examples of this.

Above: The blessing of Hall Well, Tissington

Opposite page: St Anne's Well, Buxton, 2010, celebrating 100 years of guiding

Today more well-dressings take place in Peak District villages than ever before. This may be because incomers are inspired and intrigued by this unique local custom, and are keen to join in with local people to continue the tradition into the future.

Well dressing is a real community effort, and many villagers from all walks of life are involved in the process of creating the beautiful floral icons, which can take up to 400 hours to complete.

Then when it's all over, people's thoughts turn to the possible subjects for next year's well dressing.

When did it start?

The history of well dressing

Some argue that it was the Romans who brought the custom to these shores, and they certainly worshipped the gods of certain springs and fountains. This was certainly the case at their spa town of Buxton, whose Roman name was *Aquae Arnemetiae*, or 'the spa of the goddess of the grove,' which is thought to be on the site of St Anne's Well.

After Christianity came to Britain in the 7th century, Pope Gregory instructed St Augustine to adopt pagan sites for the use of the church. Many Christian churches were built on previously pagan sites and pagan traditions were deep-seated. For example, Buxton's St Anne's Well may have been the Christian version of the Celtic goddess Anu.

An all-male line up at a Mayfield well dressing in 1896

Cyclists admire Yew Tree Well at Tissington in the early 20th century

On the instruction of Henry VIII's Lord Chancellor Thomas Cromwell, Sir William Bassett tried to put a stop to "idolatry and superstition" at Buxton by removing from St Anne's Well, a statue of St Anne and various "crutches, shirts and shifts" left there by the disabled hoping for a cure.

The pretty estate village of Tissington is generally regarded as the birthplace of the tradition in its modern form. The earliest reference to what we would recognise as well dressing at Tissington is in 1348/9, as a thanksgiving when the village escaped the deadly infestation of the Black Death, or Bubonic Plague, which had devastated the surrounding countryside.

Another event which might have revived the custom was the great drought of 1615, when Tissington's wells never ran dry despite the fact that the parish register at Youlgrave, recorded only three showers of rain in the area between the end of March and August.

The first detailed description of the custom we have is by Nicholas Hardinge, Clerk of the House of Commons, who was visiting the FitzHerbert family at Tissington Hall in 1758. He recorded "… the springs adorned with garlands; in one of these was a tablet inscribed with rhymes, composed by the schoolmaster in honour of the fountains, which, as FitzHerbert informs me, are annually commemorated upon Holy Thursday, the minister with his parishioners praying and singing over them."

Edward Rhodes records the first recognisably-modern form of well dressing in his *Peak Country* published in 1818. While most wells were decorated with wreaths and garlands of newly-gathered flowers, he adds that: "…sometimes boards are used, which are cut to the figure intended to be represented, and covered in moist clay, into which the stems of flowers are inserted… the boards thus adorned are so placed in the spring that the water appears to issue from amongst the beds of flowers."

Well dressing formerly used to be done exclusively by men, and Crichton Porteus's classic, *The Beauty and Mystery of Well-Dressing* (1949), shows a photograph of a group of men working on a vertical well dressing at Barlow and at Stoney Middleton.

Today the whole village community joins in the process of well dressing, from the young to the old and from the highest to the lowest.

Well dressing subjects

The theme of Peak District well dressings is usually religious or biblical, since the custom was adopted by the coming of Christianity to the area in Saxon times.

The themes of Tideswell's famous well-dressings are usually ecclesiastical, and a series depicting English cathedrals at the main well is particularly well regarded for its intricate detail and artistic excellence. The Shimwell family of Tideswell, led by Oliver Shimwell, were the acknowledged experts in the craft.

Momentous national events or anniversaries, such as the Golden Jubilee of Queen Victoria in 1887; her Diamond Jubilee in 1897; the Festival of Britain in 1951; the Coronation of Queen Elizabeth II in 1953; the Queen's Silver Jubilee in 1977, and the passing of the Millennium in 2000, have all been contemporary subjects for Peakland well dressings.

Other subjects have included the National Parks Awareness Campaign in 1987 at Bakewell, and the 40th anniversary of the Peak District National Park in 1991, in which 11 villages took part. They were Ashford, Bakewell, Bradwell, Buxton, Chelmorton, Cressbrook, Etwall, Litton, Monyash, Wirksworth and Youlgrave.

Other more diverse subjects have included the first landing on the Moon (at Mayfield in 1999); King Arthur's Round Table (Children's Well at Litton in 2000); packhorse routes across the Pennines (Chapel-en-le-Frith in 1999); Noddy and Big Ears – celebrating the centenary of the birth of Enid Blyton – (Ashford-in-the-Water in 1997) and even the computer game Pokemon (at Foolow in 2000).

More controversial subjects have included Arbor Low, the pagan prehistoric stone circle and henge, at Youlgrave, and various depictions of the Green Man, or the spirit of nature. This has attracted the displeasure of some religious and church authorities, despite the fact that the custom had its origin in pagan times.

Opposite page: Greaves Lane Well, Ashford-in-the-Water, 1997, celebrating the birth of Enid Blyton

Top left: Youlgrave Reading Room Well Dressing, 2010 **Top right:** Middle Well, Hollow Lane, Mayfield, 2000 **Above left:** Bakewell, All Saints Church Well Dressing, 2009 **Above right:** Stoney Middleton, 2010

Opposite page: Izaak Walton and The Compleat Angler was commemorated in Hartington's Main Well Dressing in 2009

HOW IS IT DONE?

Puddling and petalling

There is much discussion among village well dressing committees about what the subject for the following year's well dressing might be. This can take place up to a year in advance of the dressing.

Once the subject has been decided, the design of the dressing is first drawn out and then traced full-size onto tracing paper, usually by one of the more artistic members of the community.

Then the wooden frame which holds the well dressing panels is taken out of storage and carried to the local river or stream where it is submerged for several

Above: Applying the clay to the wooden frames and smoothing over the surface

Left: "Puddling" the clay

days, to ensure it soaks up and retains as much moisture as possible during the period of the standing of the dressing. In Tissington this is done in the village pond.

Next, wet clay obtained from a local quarry or stream is "puddled," usually by trampling underfoot, to make it pliable and salt is added. The puddling was traditionally done in an old tin bath or tank where it was worked with hands or feet until it was smooth and the right consistency. Getting the right consistency is a matter of experience; too wet and the clay will fall off the boards, too dry and it will not hold the petals in place.

The puddling is usually the opportunity for local schoolchildren to become involved, and like all children, they love getting messy – or "clarted-up" – with the sticky clay as they tread it down to make it soft and workable.

The clay is then pressed firmly into place on the boards and smoothed over to create a good, even surface. The placing and smoothing of the clay, which is "keyed in" by hundreds of protruding nails on the back of the boards, is a job for the adults, and the skill of a plasterer is required.

Opposite page: Wooden frames soaking in the village pond at Tissington

Now the paper template of the design is "pricked out" onto the wet clay, using a pin wheel, awl or other sharp instrument. Once the paper is removed the pricked-out design is then carefully outlined in the clay using black alder cones, seeds or black wool. Most villages frown on the use of anything other than naturally-found materials, and the collection of the required alder cones – known as "black knobs" and usually obtained from riverside trees – is just as important as the collection of flower petals and the other materials.

Top, above left & right: "Pricking out", Townhead Well, Eyam 2010
Above right: A close up of the "black knobs" being applied to the clay

Opposite page: Outlining the design, Eyam, 2010

Villagers are sent out to scour the surrounding countryside for the seeds, cones, flower petals, lichens, bark and other natural materials for colouring-in the dressing. For some effects, locally-found fluorspar is crushed and also used. Some colours are more difficult to find in the summer, particularly blue flowers, and sometimes nocturnal expeditions are made to the flower markets of nearby cities to obtain the necessary colours from flowers such as delphiniums and hydrangeas.

The real art of well-dressing is in the "petalling" or "flowering", as villagers gather to carefully press down into the clay overlapping flower petals, mosses, lichens, grass and rushes to colour in and shade the design. Usually only the pressure of the finger tips is used, but sometimes a small peg is employed. The petals are overlapped like the slates on a roof, the top one over the one below, to make it easier for rainwater to run off during the all-too-frequent showers of a Peakland summer.

The flesh tones of figures are notoriously difficult to reproduce, but natural materials which can be used include pieces of eggshell. Some well dressings leave the hands and faces of the figures as bare clay, but this can often be the first part to crack in the sun.

Above and opposite page: "Petalling" at the Eyam Town End Well Dressing, 2010

Above: Details of the "petalling" at the Eyam Town End Well Dressing, 2010

Watching petalling underway has been compared with watching several giant jigsaw puzzles being completed all at once. Most petalling is done with the panels laid out flat and horizontal, but some villages such as those at Litton, Holymoorside and Barlow seem to prefer working with the panels in a vertical position.

Finally, the boards are taken out and erected near the village well, spring, water tap or pump, usually the night before the wells are to be blessed by the local clergyman. They are then roped off and a collecting box is placed nearby, usually to raise money for a charity.

The dressings usually stand for about a week, to be admired by thousands of visitors, before they eventually start to fade, crack and disintegrate. They are watered every day in times of hot weather in order to keep them fresh.

What's involved

A time-and-motion study at a 1980s Wirksworth well dressing produced the following statistics:

400 hours was the total time taken; 80 people worked on the dressing; 3,000 nails were used on the frame; 5 cwt (a quarter of a ton or 227 kg) of clay was used; 10 cups of salt were added

And used in the flowering were:

10,000 flower petals; 80 yards of cones; 3,500 leaves; 3,800 bits of corn; 7 jars of seeds; 6 buckets of parsley and spurge

Above: Erecting the Eyam Town End Well Dressing, 2010

This is an alphabetical list of the best-known well dressings in the Peak District and surrounding area. Please note the dates of the dressings can change from year to year. It is always a good idea to check in advance with your local Tourist Information Centre for current dates.

Villagers often welcome visitors to watch the well dressing in progress, which takes place up to a week before the actual dressings are erected. Again, check locally for details.

Ashford-in-the-Water

The pretty riverside village of Ashford-in-the-Water is renowned for its picturesque Sheepwash Bridge, and one of the wells is situated under the shelter near the bridge which once protected the village water pump. A sheep washing demonstration was formerly held at the bridge on the first day of the well dressings.

Ashford's five or six well dressings are erected on the Saturday before Trinity Sunday in May, echoing the dedication of the village's medieval parish church to the Holy Trinity. The custom was revived in 1930 and 1954, and is now well established. Many people's favourite is the Children's Well, erected in Greaves Lane.

Bakewell

The popular well dressings in the Peak's 'capital' town are thought to have started in the 18th century. This was when the Duke of Rutland was attempting to capitalise on the town's warm springs to make it a spa to rival the Duke of Devonshire's nearby Buxton.

The custom was revived in 1971 and now four wells – two in Bath Gardens; one near the Butter Market in King Street, and one in South Church Street – are dressed to coincide with the town's carnival – the largest in Derbyshire – in June.

Bradwell

Bradwell's well dressings are unusual because instead of pricking the outlines of the design from the paper onto the clay, the dressers cut out a section line-by-line using razor blades. Then they petal that section before exposing the next, thus keeping the clay moist.

The four Bradwell well dressings are erected on the Saturday before the first Saturday in August to coincide with the village carnival and gala, which is held on the Beggar's Plot Playing Field. There are dressings erected at the Townend, Church Street, Smalldale and there is also a Children's Well.

Buxton

As explained earlier, Buxton's St Anne's Well may have seen the genesis of well-worshipping in the Peak 2,000 years ago in pre-Christian times.

Left: Eyam, Town End Well Dressing, 2010 **Middle:** Creesbrook, Village Green Well Dressing, 2008 **Right:** Bradwell, Town End Well Dressing, 2009

Today the Buxton wells – St Anne's Well in The Crescent; in the Market Place, and the Children's Well in Spring Gardens – are dressed on the second Sunday of July to coincide with the Buxton Music Festival and the town's carnival.

As at Youlgrave and Wirksworth, it is thought the modern custom was revived in 1840 when the Devonshire's elegant Georgian spa town first received its public water supply.

Chesterfield

It is thought that tap dressings took place in the industrial town of Chesterfield on the eastern edge of the Peak during the 19th century. The modern custom, now held at the Peacock Centre in Low Pavement, was not revived (with help from the Holymoorside dressers) until 1991. The Chesterfield wells are erected on the first Saturday of September.

Cressbrook

The former pretty cotton mill hamlet, in the Valley of the Wye just upstream from Monsal Head, erects its well dressing on the second Sunday in June, to coincide with its Gala Day.

Eyam

Eyam dresses three of its wells or springs on the Saturday prior to the last Sunday in August, which coincides with the Plague Commemoration Service in Cucklett Delf and the village carnival. The late date of the well dressings means that the choice of flowers available for the Eyam dressers is often limited, but the designs are always interesting and attract large numbers of visitors.

The largest well dressing in Eyam is the Town Head Well, which has one of the biggest screens (nine feet wide by nearly six feet tall) in the Peak. The theme of the technically-excellent Eyam well dressings often commemorates the dreadful but never-to-be forgotten visitation of the Plague in 1665/66.

Above left: Stoney Middleton, Main Well Dressing, 2008 **Middle:** Middleton by Youlgrave, 2010 **Right:** Tideswell, 2010

Left: Hartington's Main Well Dressing, 2009

Great Hucklow

Two wells are dressed on the second Thursday in August, just before the former lead mining village's Gala Day.

Great Longstone

The village school at Great Longstone is responsible for the village well dressing, which coincides with the village fete on the second Saturday of July.

Hartington

Traditionally the last of the Peak District's well dressings, Hartington's ceremony takes place on the second Saturday of September, during the village's Wakes Week. Lying as it does at the head of Dovedale in the heart of the White Peak, it is surprising to learn that Hartington's well dressings only started in 1980.

There are two wells, the main well in the Chapel driveway, and the Children's Well at the corner of School Lane.

Hope

Hope gave its name to the scenic Hope Valley, and was once a more important settlement than nearby Castleton. Its three well dressings coincide with the village carnival and Wakes Week on the first Saturday nearest to June 24 and the dressings were revived in 1949.

Middleton-by-Youlgrave

The Middleton well dressings were only started in 1977, on the occasion of the Queen's Silver Jubilee. They have continued ever since, with a single well being erected in the spacious village square on the Saturday prior to the Spring Bank Holiday in late May.

Monyash

Erected on the Saturday prior to the Spring Bank Holiday in May, Monyash dresses up to five wells, including two boards by children from the local school. The Newton Well was the first to be dressed in Monyash in 1974, when villagers from nearby Litton helped to revive the custom.

The well dressing at Monyash coincides with a village market on the green on Spring Bank Holiday Monday.

Over Haddon

Two wells are dressed at Over Haddon, the village which overlooks beautiful Lathkill Dale, on the Saturday before the late Spring Bank Holiday in May.

Stoney Middleton

The Bath Garden Well at Stoney Middleton is next to the Bath House, which was erected by local resident, Thomas Denham, Lord Chief Justice of England, in 1815 on the site of what he thought was a Roman bath house. So it may continue a very ancient celebration.

There are two other wells, both erected in The Nook near the village's uniquely octagonal Georgian parish church of St Martin's. The well dressings are held on the Saturday (usually the third) after the end of the school summer term in July.

Tideswell and Litton

The splendid 14th century parish church of Tideswell – known as the Cathedral of the Peak – is dedicated to St John the Baptist, so the village well dressings are erected on the Saturday nearest to St John the Baptist's Day, June 24. This coincides with the village Wakes Week and Carnival.

The custom was revived by the head teacher, Oliver Shimwell, at the village primary school in 1946. He was also responsible for re-introducing the ancient skills to many other Peakland villages. Tideswell's four well dressings traditionally specialise in detailed architectural subjects, particularly British churches and cathedrals, and are widely renowned for their high artistic quality.

Litton's well dressings started in 1969, with the assistance of Oliver Shimwell, to celebrate the village school's centenary. They coincide with those of nearby Tideswell. Unusually, the main picture is designed in an upright position.

Tissington

Generally-regarded as the mother of all modern well dressings and first recorded in 1758, Tissington's six wells were traditionally the first of the season. They are dressed to coincide with Ascension Day in May. Although others, such as

Wirksworth and Monyash, have superseded it today, the Peakland well dressing season is generally not thought to have begun before those in the pretty estate village of Tissington are unveiled.

The wells which are dressed are Yew Tree, Hall, Hands, Coffin, Town and the later addition in 1982 of a Children's well. This, like other children's wells elsewhere, usually attracts a lot of attention from visitors.

Wirksworth

Up to about nine wells are dressed at Wirksworth, from the Saturday before the late Spring Bank Holiday in late May/early June, to coincide with the town's carnival. The custom was revived here under the name of "tap dressings" in 1827. This was to celebrate the arrival of a piped water supply, as at Youlgrave, and the dressings were originally erected where the street taps stood.

A competition once held among Wirksworth well dressings was soon abandoned, and a team of dressers who put glass eyes in their figures, was disqualified.

Youlgrave

The modern revival of well dressings in Youlgrave was first recorded in 1829. This was when piped water was laid on for the first time to a series of taps in the village by the village's own water supply company (which still exists).

A total of five taps – Coldwell, Church Well, The Fountain (the circular water cistern in the centre of the village), Holywell Lane and Bank Top – are currently dressed on the Saturday nearest to St John the Baptist's Day, June 24.

Youlgrave's well dressings were revived again in the 1950s, by Margaret Fell and Fred Shimwell and are renowned for their high artistic content.

Well dressings further afield

Well dressing was once almost exclusively a Peak District custom, but in modern times it has spread to neighbouring counties and even further afield. Well dressings are now held in Staffordshire at Brewood, Burton-upon-Trent, Endon, Lichfield and Newborough; in South Yorkshire at Dore, Harthill and Penistone; and at Gee Cross, Sutton Lane Ends, High Legh and Macclesfield in Greater Manchester and Cheshire.

Similar customs also happen elsewhere in Britain, for example at Headon and Pleasley in Nottinghamshire; Caistor in Lincolnshire; Brescot in Shropshire and Paulton in Somerset. The Malvern Spa Association also holds a Well Dressing Weekend in May, when up to 20 wells are decorated in and around the Worcestershire spa town, and some have Peak District-style well dressing boards.

Also in May there is an Ascension Day Well Dressing at Bisley in Gloucestershire, although in this case, the dressings do not take the typical Derbyshire form of pictorial petalled boards.

Opposite page: Tissington, Coffin Well, 1997

FURTHER INFORMATION

Ashbourne Tourist Information Centre, 13 Market Place, Ashbourne, Derbyshire DE6 1EU; ☎ 01335 343666; www.visitpeakdistrict.com; open: Mar–Oct, closed Sun Nov–Feb.

Bakewell Visitor Centre, The Old Market Hall, Bridge Street , Bakewell, Derbyshire DE45 1DS; ☎ 01629 816558; www.peakdistrict.gov.uk; open daily.

Buxton Tourist Information Centre, The Crescent, Buxton SK17 6BQ; ☎ 01298 25106; www.highpeak.gov.uk; open daily.

Castleton Visitor Centre, Buxton Road , Castleton, Hope Valley S33 8WN , ☎ 01629 816558; www.peakdistrict.gov.uk; open daily. Also includes the museum of the Castleton Historical Society.

Chesterfield Tourist Information Centre, Rykneld Square, Chesterfield S40 1SB; ☎ 01246 345777/8; www.visitchesterfield.info; open daily.

Matlock Bath Tourist Information Point, Peak District Mining Museum, The Pavilion, Matlock Bath, DE4 3NR; ☎ 01629 583388; www.visitpeakdistrict.com; open daily.

Matlock Tourist Information Centre, Crown Square, Matlock, Derbyshire DE4 3AT; ☎ 01629 583388; www.visitpeakdistrict.com; open daily.

Peak District National Park

Peak District National Park Authority, Aldern House, Baslow Road, Bakewell, Derbyshire DE45 1AE; ☎ 01629 816200; www.peakdistrict.gov.uk

Published by **Ashbourne Editions**
Moor Farm Road West, Ashbourne, Derbyshire DE6 1HD
Tel: (01335) 347349 Fax: (01335) 347303

1st edition: ISBN: 978-1-873-775-39-4

© Roly Smith 2011

Printed
Gomer Press, Llandysul, Wales

Design
Mark Titterton – www.ceibagraphics.co.uk

Photography
© Mark Titterton p.2, p.8 bottom-left, p.12 top; bottom left & middle, p.13, p.14, p.15, p.16 all, p.17 all, p.19 left, p.20 top-right & bottom, back cover all

© Glyn Williams – www.welldressing.com p.8 top-left & bottom-right, p.19 middle & right, p.20 top-left & middle

© Lindsey Porter p.1, p.3, p.4, p.5, p.7, p.8 top right, p.10, p.11 all, p.12 bottom-right, p.22

© Hedley Alcock Front cover

Front Cover: Tissington, Coffin Well, 2010 **Back cover top (l-r):** Flowers stand ready for the dressers – Eyam; Head board – Town End Well, Eyam, 2010; "Petalling" **Back cover main:** "Petalling" – Town End Well Dressing, Eyam, 2010 **Page one:** Tissington, Yew Tree Well, 1998